# Answers
## for the sport parent

by Mel Roustio

TEPCA Publishing Co.
3991 Greenridge Dr.
Decatur, IL 62526
(217) 877-2089
Coachmeldec@aol.com

*99 Answers for the Sport Parent* is written by Mel Roustio of Decatur, Illinois. Mel is a parent and grandparent. He has served as a teacher, a coach, an athletic director, an umpire, a baseball scout and a fan of the games that children play. For the past few years he has conducted clinics for the training of coaches, and seminars for parents and athletes. The contents of this book represent his opinion about the questions most often asked by those involved in competitive athletics.

Mel is the author of *Courtside Memories,* a collection of stories about Illinois basketball, published by The Consortium Publishing Company in 1998.

2003 TEPCA Publishing Co.
Editor: Robert L. Crowe
Library of Congress Control Number: 2002109734
Printed by Production Press, Jacksonville, IL
4   5   6   7   8   9   10

## DEDICATION

This book is dedicated:

To my parents, Bud and Lou, whose love and support stopped short of worship;

To my wife, Gerry, who has been my partner in this coaching passion;

To Steve, Dawn, and Pam who harbor no resentment towards a father they shared with hundreds of youngsters;

To the twelve grandchildren drawn to competitive sports. May you find enjoyment and lasting lessons;

To millions of coaches who serve as teachers and caretakers,

And

To forty million youngsters who play on fields of dreams, and their parents who hope, rejoice, and agonize over every play.

# INTRODUCTION

Parents will document the countless number of "firsts" that their child negotiates. Joys are experienced watching the children play. Some children will be introduced to organized sport. Let the games begin. A proud moment occurs when the child is chosen as one of the best in the school and is part of a team.

In another place, a young adult calls his parents to share exciting news. He has been hired as a teacher/coach. His parents are happy because they know that their son will be the absolute model for the coaching profession.

These two scenarios underscore the universal conviction: no child ever envisions being a failure, and no mother ever gave birth to one. These courses ... built on confidence and love ... often become collision courses between athletes, coaches and parents.

I spent thirty-nine years coaching four different sports in six Illinois communities. My experiences include towns of a few thousand population, to cities of eighty thousand. Regardless of the community there exists one common denominator: parents want the best for their children. Therein lays the potential collision. If sport is to render a positive experience, then all involved must attempt to resolve the abundance of concerns that arise with every tick of the clock.

Every year ten million youngsters engage in competitive school sports. Millions more are in youth programs. The experience of each child will be based upon the contributions of coaches, teachers, parents, the athlete ... and fans.

This book offers 99 answers to some the frequently asked questions. This book is intended to provide a broad picture of the process. If the parent can enjoy their role, they will have the opportunity to provide their children with the experiences they all anticipate.

# 99 ANSWERS FOR THE SPORT PARENT

*(Some of the questions and responses are specifically directed to boys or girls. The remainder of the references could refer to either sex. The pronoun "he" is used in a generic sense to avoid constant clutter with "he/she" indicators.)*

## 1. WHAT ARE THE PROS AND CONS OF "EQUAL-PLAYING TIME" AND AT WHAT AGE IS IT NO LONGER AN ISSUE?

Youngsters at the introductory level of sports programs get equal opportunity and approximate equal playing time.

By the time children reach the middle-school age, the equal-playing time debate should end. Some children have more natural ability and some practice more intently to develop athletic abilities. Those youngsters with superior skills are rewarded with more playing time.

There is a reason for keeping score. In the process of assessing capabilities, all students will not receive the same academic grades; all athletes will not receive an equal amount of playing time.

## 2. MOST SCHOOLS HAVE TRY-OUTS RESULTING IN KIDS BEING CUT FROM THE TEAM. DO EDUCATORS REALIZE HOW TRAUMATIC THIS EXPERIENCE CAN BE FOR YOUNGSTERS?

Coaches should structure the try-out experience to minimize the disappointment the youngsters feel.

Administrators should have conversations with their coaches and insist upon team selection procedures that minimize the negative impact for the student who fails to make the team. A squad "cut" policy might include the following elements: (1) a letter sent prior to try-outs to parents defining factors that limit the final squad number. For example, the size of the team might be limited to 15 players (2) an outline of sport-specific skills to be observed and the grading manner (3) multiple try-out sessions, and (4) a personal conversation with each youngster not making the team in lieu of a publicly posted "cut list."

Parents and students should understand that team composition must be considered. For example, a football coach cannot keep fifteen 150 pound running backs, regardless of how good they may be. There are other factors to be considered in assessing the talents of the other positions.

Not everyone makes the team and coaches do sometimes miss in their evaluations. It is reasonable, however, to believe that the coach wants to keep the best players.

# 3. AT WHAT AGE SHOULD MY CHILD BEGIN PARTICIPATION IN ORGANIZED SPORTS?

Competitive participation usually begins between the ages of 5 and 10. The decision when to begin a child in sports should not be made solely upon age.

The long standing debate regarding age and organized sports has two distinct camps. One philosophy suggests early competition while the other approach embraces "free-play" with natural evolvement into competition.

The argument will not be soon resolved because there are numerous examples of success using both methods. The key words are "organized" and "competitive" and how they are perceived by parent and child. "Organized" suggests structured learning with safety. The term "competitive" suggests aggression and pressure.

Competition isn't a negative condition. When youngsters play they usually gravitate to a challenge. Who runs the fastest? Who throws the rock the farthest? Who can climb highest on the playground apparatus? Parents would be wise to take "cues" from their children. As you observe your child at play in various games, note the ability to run, throw, kick and catch.

Children 5 to 8 years old develop one-dimensional tracking. An example of this is the ability to hit a baseball from a stationary tee (T-Ball). Two-dimensional tracking in the brain begins at about eight years of age. An example of this is the ability to hit a moving (pitched) ball.

Observe the child in terms of their physical abilities including coordination. Make note of the child's temperament as he responds to his success and failures. How do they react to the competitive environment? Do they enjoy the activity?

The astute parent is in the position to interpret the signals and decide the child's readiness.

## 4. WHAT ARE THE BENEFITS OF SPORT PARTICIPATION AS CLAIMED BY SPORT ADVOCATES?

The celebration around sport participation renders many claims of abundant goodness. It has been suggested that sport builds character, sport reflects society, and sport prepares participants to meet life challenges. Sport may do many good things, but it is not automatic.

The rewards occur when the individual sees the gap closing between present abilities and his potential. He then recognizes the benefits of commitment, of following instructions, practicing skill development, working hard to achieve a goal, playing by the rules, self discipline and role-playing as it relates to the needs of the group.

The greatest outcome from sport participation is the blueprint it leaves for the individual to follow in living experiences beyond the "play" arenas.

The sport experience will help the individual to ask the larger question: "What can I do for the good of family, community, church, and others?"

4

## 5. IS IT WISE FOR PARENTS TO COACH THEIR OWN CHILDREN IN YOUTH PROGRAMS?

If it were not for the volunteer parent coaches, youth programs would close shop.

The parent-coach likely will have empathy for other children and the other parents. Likewise, they are probably more dependable and more focused on taking care of children than in developing a sports program.

A downside possibility is that the parent-coach runs the risk of resentment from parents and players who may perceive the coach as favoring his own child. If a parent coaches his own child over a prolonged period of time, the child is deprived of experiences found in different personalities and coaching methods.

The success of youth programs hinges upon the support and involvement of parents. Every parent should look for ways to help. Many parents should take their turn coaching teams. However ... don't take <u>every</u> turn.

## 6. IS THERE A UNIVERSAL SPORT PHILOSOPHY APPLICABLE TO YOUTH PROGRAMS?

Yes. *The American Sports Education Program*, a nationally recognized coaching certification curriculum program, states it best: "athletes first, winning second." This philosophy does not de-emphasize competing to win, but primarily takes into consideration the athlete's development and welfare.

## 7. SHOULD I BE CONCERNED WITH THE INCREASE IN VIOLENCE IN SPORTS?

You bet! We should all be concerned about the increase in sports violence. There are two dimensions: violence by players and violence by fans. Both dimensions can be addressed at the same time.

Parents and program leaders should establish pro-active measures that specify acceptable behaviors and the consequences. Mandatory pre-season meetings between players, coaches and officials should result in written expectations. There should be clear statements of warnings and subsequent actions for violators of the standards. Then ... somebody has to have the authority and the courage to enforce the provisions.

## 8. WILL SPORT PARTICIPATION HELP MY CHILD'S SELF-ESTEEM?

Perhaps.

Self-esteem is pride in oneself ... self-respect.

When a child works hard to develop a sport skill and can successfully apply the skill, he develops self-esteem. He feels good about himself and the accomplishment.

Let's take another scenario. If a child participates in a sport and develops little or no skills, makes constant errors, and is embarrassed with his play ... no self esteem is present.

One of the responsibilities of a coach is to assist with skill development. Through accomplishment, self esteem can be generated.

## 9. OUR YOUTH TEAMS GIVE OUT A <u>LOT</u> TROPHIES AND AWARDS. IS THIS GOOD?

It's expensive. Sports awards are given more freely today, not only in youth leagues but also in many adult leagues. We have become an award/recognition society.

Some organizations give everyone an award in an effort to create self-esteem. Awards do not convey self-esteem. Participation awards are fine. However, giving everyone on a team an award regardless of individual merit diminishes the awards and does not achieve the intent. After a brief instant of warm-fuzzy feelings for the child and the parent, the award has no value. It is not tied to an accomplishment. The child may be proud of the award just as he is proud of his bicycle ... but it is not self-esteem. Awards should be predicated upon real achievement.

## 10. WE HEAR THE SPORT CLICHÉ, "IT'S NOT IF YOU WIN OR LOSE BUT HOW YOU PLAY THE GAME." IF IT'S NOT ABOUT WINNING, THEN WHY DO WE PLAY COMPETITIVE SPORT AND KEEP SCORE?

Winning ... at any price? By any means? Players use skills to compete within a boundary of rules and civil behavior. Winning should be attained within those boundaries.

There are players who win by breaking the rules or using unfair equipment. They cannot beat their opponent using game skills so they violate the integrity of the game. But it's a "win."

We increasingly see athletes who win and do "in-your-face" insults or "trash-talk." Most observers believe such actions diminish the status of the winner.

There are many benefits of playing the game and enjoying the process even when you don't win every game. Every player will win some and lose some but for the real winners ... it's how you play the game.

## 11. I AM UPSET WITH MY SON'S COACH BUT FEAR A CONVERSATION MIGHT RESULT IN HIM RESENTING MY SON. WHAT CAN I DO?

If your child was having academic difficulties in school, would you hesitate contacting his teacher to seek insight into the problem? If your child continued to experience tooth pain long after a visit with the dentist, would you not arrange for a return visit to look into the matter? The answers to these questions are obvious.

The concern you have regarding your son's coach retaliating because of a conversation should not enter your mind. Of course, it depends upon your manner of inquiry. Like other people, coaches usually become defensive when attacked.

By all means call the coach and arrange a time to chat face to face. Make sure you're seeking answers to questions which will ultimately enhance your child's sport experiences. Be prepared to hear someone with a different perspective express objective opinions about your child.

## 12. IS ONE PARTICULAR COACHING "STYLE" MORE EFFECTIVE?

About the time you argue that one style is more effective, a host of exceptions comes to mind. There is no one way to coach. We can generalize that there are three basic coaching styles: dominant, permissive and democratic.

The dominant coach might be viewed as "my way or the highway." The dominant coach perceives his role as military authoritative, not to be challenged or questioned. There have been and are many successful dominant style coaches. One problem with dominant coaches is they may stifle potentially valuable input from players or assistants that could be beneficial to the cause.

At the opposite end of the spectrum we find the "permissive style" coach, laid back with seemingly no urgency. Sometimes there is a question as to who is in charge. The players seem to take the lead on how the game proceeds.

One word can best define the democratic style: "ownership." The democratic coach makes the ultimate final decisions but he invites input into preparations from his staff and athletes. This style of coaching promotes the "ownership" feeling. That is, the process isn't a coach ordering around a bunch of robots, nor the players emerging out of chaos, but a joint participation. Those who feel ownership in any organization tend to give more effort for the ultimate success. I believe the "democratic coaching style" holds greater promise for both fun and success.

## 13. MY SON'S COACH YELLS AT THE PLAYERS. IS THAT NECESSARY?

In addition to different coaching styles, it is obvious that there are personality differences among coaches. Listen to the content of what is being yelled. Some coaches have personalities that are likely louder than the more soft spoken coach. Certainly, parents are not offended if the coach is yelling encouragement or praise towards their youngster. On sports teams, there is usually an understanding between coach and player that the intent of all communication is improvement. Players usually handle this constructive criticism very well ... whatever the tone. Coaching is much like parenting. Children know the intent of mom and dad's manner of communication and filter the tone or volume. The same is likely true with their coach. The key lies in the intent. Coaches should never direct demeaning comments or personal attacks at any player, publicly or privately. If so, the parent should communicate the concern to the coach or administrative body.

**14. MY SON DOES NOT SHARE MUCH INFORMATION OR FEELINGS ABOUT HIS TEAM. HOW CAN I GET MORE INFORMATION FROM HIM?**

It is a legitimate expectation to want children to share information.

One idea … make inquiries specific. Teenagers wish to short-circuit conversations with parents. If you ask, "How is school going?" or "How does the team look?" you will likely get an "ok" response. A better inquiry might be, "What are you studying in history?" or "What kind of defensive approach is the team taking this season?"

Composing good questions will assist in developing communication.

**15. THE HIGH SCHOOL COACH SOCIALIZES WITH THE "COUNTRY CLUB" SET IN OUR TOWN AND HIS COACHING DECISIONS OFTEN REFLECT FAVORITISM TOWARDS THE WEALTHY KIDS.**

The coach should appreciate the fact that he is perceived as the high school's coach … and the community's coach. He belongs to all. If the coach can always be found in the bars after games his image will be questioned in the conservative circles. Should he always align himself with the country club set, he may be viewed as too "uppity" for the masses. In smaller communities the activities and social interaction of the coach are more than casually noted. There will always be some group that says, "He doesn't socialize with us."

The coach's job is to select a team and win games. His continued employment depends upon that simple statistic. Coaches select participants that are the best players ... regardless of railroad tracks, addresses, and checking balances.

## 16. WHY DO EDUCATORS ENCOURAGE PARENTS TO GET INVOLVED IN THEIR CHILD'S EDUCATION AND THEN SHOW RESENTMENT WHEN QUESTIONED ABOUT TEACHING OR COACHING METHODS?

This is one area that can be positively impacted when a sincere invitation by school personnel is met by supportive parents. Administrators and coaches should not be threatened by public questioning but view it as an opportunity to dispel rumors and misunderstandings. Often a simple explanation can eliminate confusion or hard feelings.

Sometimes school personnel ask for parental involvement and do get overly defensive when questioned. On the other side of the coin, sometimes parents will berate school personnel when their real agenda is, "Why aren't you giving my kid higher grades?" or "Why doesn't my kid get to play more?"

## 17. OUR HIGH SCHOOL TEAMS PLUG ALONG WITH CONSISTENT MEDIOCRITY. DO SCHOOL ADMINISTRATORS ATTEMPT TO IMPROVE PROGRAM QUALITY?

My definition of program quality would be "competitive teams comprised of youngsters having positive learning and enjoyable experiences." The question, however, speaks more to success as defined by winning seasons.

The following are common ingredients found in "winning" programs: (1) strong enrollment numbers (2) well planned and operated youth pro-grams (3) coordinated "feeder" programs in ele-mentary and middle schools (4) well constructed schedules that present realistic challenges (5) off-season training programs (6) administrative support (7) properly controlled parent-booster club support (8) appropriate practice and training facilities (9) com-municated guidelines of expectations of coaches and parents (10) ongoing educational opportunities for staff.

Many of the above elements are not necessary if there is simply great athletic talent. Seldom can that sustain a sports program. Most school administrators and coaches understand the above ingredients. However, too often more money is spent on equipment and not enough on programs to educate and develop the coaching ranks.

Some coaches resign or get fired because they lack the expertise in their sport, but many leave due to the periphery factors around high school sports. School administrators can do much to improve these relationship dynamics.

## 18. COSTS KEEP GOING UP TO SUPPORT MORE NEW SPORT'S PROGRAMS. WHY DO WE NEED SO MANY PROGRAMS ... AND WHATEVER BECAME OF THE COACH WHO COACHES THREE SPORTS?

You would be surprised by the small percent of a school's budget that goes to sports programs. In the last fifty years there has been a marked increase in program offerings in public schools. Some new programs resulted because of state and federal mandates and many came because parents demanded more opportunities for their children.

The whereabouts of the three sport coach? Most of the change in attitude and personnel came because of specialization. Off-season training and competition demanded that the coach spend a great deal of time in the off-season. It is also a fair assumption that sport teaching and training techniques have become more sophisticated, thus begging for specific expertise.

# 19. IS IT MY IMAGINATION OR HAS THE THREE-SPORT LETTER WINNER VANISHED FROM THE HIGH SCHOOL SCENE?

The youngster playing three sports can still be found. However, the number is greater in the smaller high schools. Three factors are now in place that were not widespread fifty years ago. First, a greater number of high school athletes are specializing in one or two sports. Good or bad this is in hopes of gaining college scholarships. Secondly, teenage employment opportunities draw scores of youngsters away from sport participation. These kids are turned on by the purchase possibilities of designer clothes and the automobile. Remember the sport student-manager ... that youngster who was always there doing countless duties to benefit the program? He is an endangered species. He took his work ethics to a fast food restaurant and gets a paycheck. Finally, every high school sport now has a playoff system which has lengthened seasons causing some unavoidable overlap. Coaches are more than happy to make cooperative arrangements to share the "star" athlete but it is usually the parents and the student who choose to specialize in one sport.

## 20. OUR HIGH SCHOOL HAS A GROWING NUMBER OF COACHES WHO ARE NOT TEACHERS. HOW CAN NON-EDUCATORS IN COACHING POSITIONS BE A SOUND EDUCATIONAL IDEA?

In a perfect world, only qualified teachers with coaching expertise would be our high school coaches. The high school sports' world has NEVER been perfect. Years ago, much care was taken to place faculty members who were trained coaches in the high profile sports such as boys' basketball and football. The other sports that many referred to as "minor" sports got left-over faculty folks. A principal would ask a teacher to do a favor and take a "minor" coaching position, and many times a new teacher with limited sport knowledge might agree to take a coaching job just to secure a teaching position. Even "the good-old days" had educator-coaches with little knowledge of a sport.

After a period of time, personnel resigned their coaching positions but remained as a teacher. Thus, there are few positions available for the hiring of coaches who are on the school faculty.

While there are less and less teaching positions available for the coaching duties, new laws and demands create more and more opportunities for children. Whoops! There is a shrinking pool of coaches and expanding programs. Who will coach our children? State associations across the nation looked to non-teachers with coaching potential. Several certification curriculum plans were developed. Most states today use this method to certify coaches. Perfect? No ... but no less perfect than days gone by. The critical charge for the school administrator today is background investigation, a well designed interview process, staff development, and a legitimate evaluation process.

## 21. MANY HIGH SCHOOL COACHING POSITIONS HAVE RAPID TURNOVER. HOW DO WE INSURE CONSISTENCY THAT LEADS TO SUCCESS?

There is no way to avoid some problems when there is constant turnover. Adjusting to new coaching personalities with a variety of styles is difficult at best. There are a few things that can be done.
1. Have a well defined and realistic athletic code.
2. Have a clear and adequate budget.
3. Have administrative procedures and support.
The idea is to create a structure so that when a new coach enters there is solid support already in place.

## 22. WHY DO COACHES CONTINUE PLAYING THE FIRST TEAM EVEN WHEN THEY ARE AHEAD BY A WIDE MARGIN?

There is no universal answer to satisfy this question but there are four considerations. First, we must recognize the various sport rules regarding substitution "re-entry." For example, the rules in baseball states that a player leaving the game for a substitution is disqualified for the remainder of the contest. On the other hand, football and volleyball players may re-enter the contest. This may impact the coaching decision to substitute. Secondly, many rule changes in some sports have redefined the "safe" lead. The three point field goal in basketball has created the opportunity for more points to be scored in a shorter period of time. This may be a concern for a coach's substitution philosophy. Thirdly, the coach may have individuals who are on pace to establish certain career milestones which beg for more playing time. Finally, the coach may simply lack the necessary trust in the reserves and thus hesitates to make those substitutions.

## 23. I HAVE SEEN A NUMBER OF MALES COACHING FEMALE TEAMS. WHY DON'T SCHOOLS RECRUIT FEMALE COACHES?

It is more a problem of supply than recruiting. There are more girls' sports and there are few female coaches. Many young women leave the coaching field for home making and child rearing. If many of the girls' sports are to continue, they will have to use male coaches ... at least until colleges and communities bolster the supply side.

## 24. IS THERE ANY DOWNSIDE TO THE EMERGENCE OF ORGANIZED YOUTH SPORTS?

Many observers bemoan the loss in leadership skills among young athletes. Youngsters are not engaged in pick-up games as in the past. When children are alone to organize their games, someone will take charge. They must choose their own teams, develop rules, and administer the game. These circumstances afford an opportunity where leadership skills are honed. When adults do all the planning, management, and officiating, the opportunity for youth leadership is removed.

Organized games with fans, uniforms, and sports facilities change the way youngsters handle themselves. When there was a pick-up baseball game on the corner lot, the emphasis seemed to be on the enjoyment of the game and not so much on the outcome.

## 25. WHY DO ATHLETIC TRAINING RULES DIFFER FROM SCHOOL TO SCHOOL?

State-wide rules tend to address eligibility but local schools can define their own standards of training rules ... call it "social behavior." The attitudes toward student behavior vary widely within and between communities.

Each state has a governing association that establishes and monitors sport competition. A common rule applied to all association members is that if a school declares a student athlete ineligible because of a training rules infraction, the student may not move into another district and circumvent the punishment. The student must be in good academic and social standing from the school he is leaving.

## 26. HOW SHOULD A PARENT HANDLE THE PRESSURES AND DISAPPOINTMENT THEIR CHILD FACES IN COMPETITIVE SPORTS?

It is important that parents talk with their child about the highs and lows that are part and parcel to competitive sport. Sometimes the greatest baseball players strike out. Sometimes luck plays a part in who wins. Sometimes the opponent is better. Talk to your child about the experiences awaiting them in games and reinforce the premise that one that competes gives total energy and effort, then walks away accepting the outcome. Parents cannot guarantee health, happiness or success for their children. We can only give them our unconditional love. Let them play and watch them grow.

## 27. THROUGHOUT ELEMENTARY SCHOOL MY SON HAS STRUGGLED ACADEMICALLY. HE WISHES TO PARTICIPATE IN MIDDLE SCHOOL SPORTS. SHOULD I LIMIT HIS PLAY TO INSURE BETTER GRADES?

There is a huge misconception centered on sport participation and academic success. Sport demands much time and energy expenditure. Some people assume that the amount of practice time reduces time for academic study. The invalid assumption is that practice time would be devoted to studies ... that "if my child weren't practicing, he would be studying." Probably not.

State high school associations across America have academic guidelines in place that speak to minimum standards of grade achievement for the sport participant. The student's grades are monitored during his sport season. Coaches are in a position to alert parents of grade woes and also obtain faculty or peer tutoring for the struggling athlete. Due to close scrutiny and your son's desire to stay eligible you may notice improved academic grades.

## 28. I SIT IN THE STANDS AT MY DAUGHTER'S SOCCER GAMES AND HEAR VICIOUS REMARKS FROM FANS DIRECTED TOWARDS THE COACH AND PLAYERS. CAN SOMETHING BE DONE ABOUT THIS BEHAVIOR?

Absolutely! The problem is that too many people in authoritative positions are apathetic or fear to upset a patron by admonishing their behavior. Some authorities have the attitude that people pay money for a ticket and have a right to express themselves, or "parents will be parents," or "I can't do anything about fan behavior." Shouting vulgarity and harsh critical remarks at youth league contests and at school events should not be tolerated. A pre-season meeting with parents and athletes outlining crowd behavior expectations and a similar communication to the student body will do much to alert what consequences result from unacceptable actions. A public announcement prior to each contest will warn others. This must be followed-up with a no nonsense administrative policing.

## 29. WHY WON'T MY DAUGHTER'S HIGH SCHOOL COACH ALLOW HER AND OTHER PLAYERS TO RIDE HOME WITH PARENTS FROM OUT OF TOWN GAMES?

There are legal, social and team ramifications.

The school event calling for school transportation places a certified employee of the school district in charge and responsible for all students to arrive safely to and from the event.

Liability exists for the parents when friends of their child also ride along from events.

Usually, the request is made by parents who have the financial means to attend out of town games and the transportation becomes a socio-economic statement. The wealthy kids get private transportation and the poor kids ride the bus.

Perhaps the most important reason for players to ride the bus to and from contest is found in the significant learning experience. These youngsters comprise a team. They prepare together. They perform together. They win or lose together … and they interact and process as they ride the bus together.

There are circumstances that arise that should permit a student to ride with his parents. Those situations are rare and limited.

## 30. ISN'T IT UNFAIR AND UNWISE TO PLAY A FRESHMEN OR A SOPHOMORE AHEAD OF A SENIOR ON THE VARSITY TEAM?

The selection of team members is based upon who has the skills to make the greatest contribution. It is not based upon age, social standing or parent interference.

In team sports, we must keep in mind that there are various skills needed for various roles. In *individual* sports the statistics dictate much in the coach's decision. The years I coached cross-country, I was never uncertain which seven runners would be entered in the meet. The stop watch the day before told me.

Few observers would advocate that each year the team must be comprised of seniors. If your son were the sophomore with clearly superior skills, would you advocate that the older players get selected? The above question has been asked many times … and it is always the parent of the senior.

## 31. I HAVE NOTICED JEALOUSIES AMONG MY DAUGHTER'S MIDDLE SCHOOL VOLLEYBALL TEAM. WHAT DO COACHES DO TO CORRECT THIS SITUATION?

Parents should not be too alarmed at this behavior. Chances are, if you have more than one child, you have witnessed jealousies between your very own children. In the home setting we refer to this as sibling rivalry. Whenever youngsters are gathered together under some authoritative leadership they tend to build up feelings of resentment towards one another if they perceive their own position lessened within the group. A wise coach, just like the parent, is keenly aware of the needs each individual member has to feel worthy and important.

To minimize jealousies the coach should periodically spend time in both individual and group conversations regarding the value of each team member. Focus can be given to the importance for each to accept roles and be accountable to the group. Comments to the media can often be directed towards those individuals doing the "little things" rather than the prolific scorer who would undoubtedly get attention.

## 32. MY DAUGHTER WANTS TO PLAY SPORT IN EVERY SEASON. CAN KIDS BE INVOLVED IN TOO MANY SPORTS?

It's possible. Some students can handle studies, athletics, a job, organization involvement, and a social schedule. Other students cannot. Talents as well as physical and mental capacities have to be taken into consideration.

If the parent sees warning flags such as extreme fatigue, missed responsibilities, lower grades and diminished performance, then it's time for the parent to discuss the amount of activities. Often, some type of contractual agreement can be a tool to jointly monitor the concerns.

## 33. MY SON HAS LIMITED ATHLETIC ABILITY YET HE HOPES TO PLAY SPORTS IN COLLEGE. HOW SHOULD A PARENT HANDLE THEIR CHILD'S UNREALISTIC SPORT DREAMS?

Unrealistic dreams for a child are usually held by parents. Often, those expectations translate into pressure felt by the youngster.

Most little league players collecting those bubble gum cards envision their picture on such a card. Coaches are "caretakers" of a kid's field of dreams. One technique in coaching is to get your athletes to think they are better than they really are. You remember, "I think I can, I think I can ... I know I can, I know I can." That's okay.

When the high school age athlete talks of playing college sport, it is time for candid conversation between student-athlete, parents, and coach. The coach can play a primary role discussing the abilities of the youngster in terms of what level of college sport is realistic. It should be noted that everything from Division 1 to local community junior colleges are part of the menu.

## 34. OUR SCHOOL DOESN'T GET MEDIA COVERAGE BUT A NEIGHBORING SCHOOL GETS A LOT OF INK. WHAT CAN WE DO TO GET OUR SHARE OF RECOGNITION?

City schools, rural schools, big schools and small schools all feel that they are slighted by the media. Don't take it personally. Every newspaper, radio station and TV station has a tremendous range of sports news to cover. National, state, area and local coverage in a wide variety of sports is expected by the subscribers. The sport page is expected to follow suit and give some equality to middle schools and high schools in both boy's and girl's activities. You can increase the possibility of receiving better media coverage. First, make sure all the school's coaches cooperate with every media request and be consistent with reporting scores of contests. Secondly, send weekly statistics and stories about your teams and players. This will keep your school in the minds of those doing the reporting and sooner or later the coverage is forthcoming.

## 35. WHAT IS THE PRIMARY COACHING RESPONSIBILITY IN A TEAM SPORT?

I think the primary responsibility is to assess the abilities of the team members, and of the team as a group. Determining the strengths and weaknesses of an individual will allow the shaping of developmental skills and exercises. Assessing the forté and weakness of a team allows focused practices for improvement.

Knowing strengths allows the coach to design game strategies that use the best abilities. Knowing weaknesses permits meaningful exercises for improvement.

## 36. DO YOU SEE ANY COMMON WEAKNESS IN TODAY'S SCHOOL COACHES?

Yes. Too often coaches lack communication skills. They need to communicate expectations in direct and simple terms. This statement of expectations will go far to eliminate the response by students and parents, "I didn't know."

Often the coaches are architects of complex and confusing strategies. Coaches study their sport, scout opponents, and spend endless hours planning. They need to remind themselves: "Keep it simple, stupid." My middle school track coach told us just prior to a race, "Boys, keep turning left and hurry back."

It is important that young athletes get into a performance "flow" and they can only do this when they understand the system.

## 37. WHY IS IT THAT MY SON'S SCHOOL HAS FAR FEWER "PEP" ASSEMBLIES THAN I REMEMBER AS A HIGH SCHOOL PLAYER?

Three main reasons:
1. Academic time loss. Many teachers are sensitive to the loss of  class time and are quick to express displeasure to administrators.

2. Political correctness. When a school has a number of sports it is necessary to give equal consideration to assemblies. Other clubs and organizations often want similar recognition.

3. Monitoring the jerks. A problem usually arises with the youngsters who don't want to be in school at all. They look for opportunities to skip or disrupt ... the school assembly offers both.

## 38. HOW SHOULD A COACH PROCESS A CONCERN BY AN UNHAPPY PARENT?

Some student-athletes and parents will at times be unhappy with the coach during the season. It is inevitable and it usually centers on lack of playing time. The communication process should not be a difficult issue for the coach. The school with proper administrative leadership should have a policy addressing this matter well in place.

Schools require a pre-season physical examination for the athlete. Schools should also require every sport to hold a pre-season meeting with required attendance of coaches, parents and the athlete. At the meeting the athletic code is reviewed and signed by parent and student-athlete, thus engaging the front-end of "due process." The coach should outline the specific expectations in his sport and communicate what all parties can expect. Matters pertaining to grades, practice sites and times, transportation, injuries, and excused practices should be defined. It should be stated that sport is not an equal opportunity situation. Some students will get more playing time than others.

Specific mention should be made about the process if the student or parent is unhappy. Such a process might be as follows: The parent contacts the head coach to set up a meeting and the student athlete must be at that meeting. Two coaches will listen very carefully to the concerns expressed by parents and athlete. The coaches will outline the strengths and weaknesses of the athlete indicating what they perceive to be the current role and projected future role. No other athletes will be discussed during this meeting. Often, issues can be resolved with the exchange of information. In more serious matters, the athlete must ultimately make the choice to leave the team or remain a member.

## 39. SHOULD I ALLOW MY DAUGHTER TO QUIT HER HIGH SCHOOL SOCCER TEAM?

Yes, if that's what she wants to do. Can you imagine her having success and enjoyment if she goes to practice only because you order her to do so? The first step is to find out why she no longer wishes to participate. Does she merely need someone to prop-up her confidence? Does she have a misplaced definition of success? Is there a personality conflict that might be resolved?

There are some players who should not see the season through to conclusion. Some kids hate the sport, hate the coach, don't want to practice, etc. In the main ... if the student doesn't want to play ... how much pressure should the parent give?

## 40. HOW VALUABLE ARE SPORT CAMPS?

Sport camps are usually a wonderful experience for youngsters. They meet new people and learn new wrinkles to their sport. The sport camp won't send home a vastly improved athlete any more than a piano teacher will produce an accomplished performer after a few lessons. Camps don't develop athletes. Athletes are developed through endless hours of skill practice and training. Camps can help provide additional opportunity for development.

## 41. IS IT WISE TO LET MY DAUGHTER COMPETE IN TWO YOUTH LEAGUE PROGRAMS IN A ONE SEASON TIME FRAME?

Is that her idea, or yours? If she just absolutely loves both sports and refuses to give up one of them, then you may have a reason to allow her to participate. Even the best of athletes have difficulty managing practice and game time. Assuming that she also has some time to be a child ... it probably isn't a good idea.

## 42. HOW CAN I HELP MY SON OVERCOME HIS FEAR OF FAILURE?

The first problem is that a child is thinking that the results of a game represent failure.

A child's fear of failure stems from his uncertainty of how others, especially parents and peers, will view him. First, you must present a clear and realistic meaning of failure. Try to create an understanding that failure has nothing to do with making the team, starting on the team, making errors or winning games. Every sport participant should seek to understand the meaning of <u>potential</u> and <u>performance</u>. "Am I striving to be the best I can possibly be?" "Am I using my skills to the best of my ability?"

Talk with your child openly about these perceptions. Explain that all attempts in sport ... and life ... carry some risks. Things will not always turn out as we wish. Success is only possible for those who try. While running for public office, Abraham Lincoln was defeated more often than winning. The great .300 hitters in baseball did not get hits the majority of the time. Reinforce the message that the true joy in sport is found in the challenges we choose for ourselves.

## 43. WHAT IS CONSIDERED A REASONABLE AGE TO BEGIN WEIGHT TRAINING?

The theory behind weight training is that greater strength can be realized through a specifically designed, regimented workout that causes the body's muscles to contract under tension. The application of the theory is only effective if the body can accommodate the changes. Muscles are supported by bone structure. Until the age 14, those bones are susceptible to injury in "free weights" training. At about the age of 14, the child can begin a muscle development program that is carefully prescribed and monitored. Prior to this age, much can be done to develop strength through physical conditioning such as push-ups and pull-ups.

## 44.  MY SON EXCELS IN SPORTS. HOW DO I KEEP HIM FROM BECOMING THE EGOCENTRIC ATHLETE THAT IS SEEN IN COLLEGE AND THE PROS?

Most children are the product of what their parents and coaches allow them to be. Yes, there are exceptions but most behavior can be shaped.

Someone has to explain the reality of life. The child must understand that there are a lot of other athletes as good or better. Being superior in skills in your town or school does not bestow a flood of admiration in the world. In fact, their attitude may bring wide disapproval … even with their superior skills. It will be helpful to know that you, as parents, do not admire the behavior of those egocentric athletes to whom you refer.

Your son's accomplishments may be noteworthy. In sport we can be sure of one thing: he's about to meet some as good or better than he is.

## 45.  WHY DO SCHOOL ADMINISTRATORS PROTECT INCOMPETENT COACHES?

A lot of the answer is in the definition of "incompetent." You know … "the eye of the beholder." One of the responsibilities of administrators is to assure that the coach is given every opportunity to succeed.

The removal of a coach from a position

should be based upon a solid understanding of job elements. Many of the parents who shout "Incompetent!" really mean that their kid isn't getting enough playing time. Some fans who yell "Fire the bum!" mean that their tiny ego is being hurt when they talk with people in the nearby town that won the game.

There are incompetent coaches ... just as there are incompetents in other professions. A base of realistic expectations should be the criteria for retention or dismissal.

## 46. WHY DO SOME SCHOOL DISTRICTS INCLUDE TOWNSPEOPLE ON COMMITTEES TO INTERVIEW AND RECOMMEND WHEN HIRING COACHES?

I strongly oppose townspeople being part of committees to interview and recommend coaching appointments. My dissent is based upon two unsettling issues. 1. What credentials qualify committee members? 2. What message does this procedure send? Such committees are asked to engage a responsibility that is clearly a duty of educational administrators who are best qualified to assess the teaching and coaching potential. Rarely, if ever, do we find citizen committees used for all sports. Usually, a committee such as this is only used when reviewing applicants for boys' basketball and football positions at the high school level. This implied insult to other programs tends to reflect what the administrators believe to be important.

The administrative attraction to outside committee

usage is obvious. It permits ego stroking of community power bases and tends to exonerate administrators in the decision.

## 47. WHY IS OFFICIATING SO POOR IN THE MIDDLE AND HIGH SCHOOLS?

An unfortunate attitude in our society is to look upon the "umpire" as the potential villain at all sporting events. The official becomes the target should our team lose. Recognize officials as we do players, coaches, and teams ... some are good and some are not so good. It is difficult finding people who are willing to become game officials. The potential for abuse far out-weighs the pay. Every state athletic association rates the competency of officials. During state sponsored tournaments, the state sport association assigns the highest rated officials to those contests. If a school is in a conference, the participating schools usually generate a list of acceptable officials. Meaningful attempts are made by all parties to put the best officials in the game. We should applaud those people who are willing to be officials.

## 48. ARE RUNNING AND OTHER FORMS OF PHYSICAL ACTIVITY THE BEST METHOD TO SHAPE AN ATHLETE'S BEHAVIOR?

NO. The most effective method is to talk with the student and assess the reasons for negative behavior. The student should be told the effects of their behavior and the consequences if the behavior doesn't change. Coaches, teachers and parents should be involved as appropriate. Using physical activity as a punishment implies that it is a negative activity rather than a positive pursuit. Adjusting playing time is a very effective means of shaping behavior.

## 49. WHAT CAN I DO TO HELP MY CHILD WHEN SHE GETS DEPRESSED OVER HER PERFORMANCE IN GAMES?

It is important to understand the depth and seriousness of your daughter's depression as it pertains to her performance. Many youngsters simply believe they are supposed to be depressed if their team loses or if they don't turn in a good performance. Others may feel that they have let down their parents and thus show a somewhat masked depression in hopes of gaining sympathy or forgiveness. Talk with your child about her feelings and listen carefully to what is being said. Help your child keep the bigger picture in mind. Sport should reflect enjoyment and pride.

# 50. HOW DO I HANDLE A PLAYER ON MY YOUTH "TRAVELING" SOCCER TEAM WHO ARGUES AND USES PROFANITY?

If it is a continuing problem, apparently you aren't doing anything about it. The first step is that the coach must take the step to end the behavior.

In the coach-player relationship there are certain things that are non-negotiable:

Everyone will report on time.

Everyone will listen to instructions.

Everyone will work hard.

Neither profanity nor vulgarity will be tolerated.

In the late 1960's, I recall asking a player who had cursed in practice if he talked like that at home. He said, "No." and I told him he would not talk that way at practice. Sometime in the mid-1970's, a similar conversation took place with a player and his response was, "Yeh, we all cuss at my house." ... so I changed the question.

The athletic experience belongs to all and the definition of acceptable behavior must be immediately established. This policy <u>must</u> be communicated to players and parents. Warnings, follow-up conversations, meetings with organizers, administrators and parents can be a series of procedures. Suspension or removal from the team are last resort actions.

## 51. AS A MALE COACH OF A GIRLS' CLUB VOLLEYBALL TEAM SHOULD I BE CONCERNED WITH GIVING PLAYERS RIDES HOME AFTER GAMES AND PRACTICES?

The best advice I can give is to be aware of the negative possibilities. Innocent conversation can sometimes be misinterpreted by students. If there is a situation that you believe might be inappropriate, do something about it. Get another adult to ride along, find other parents to drive occasionally, vary the order that the same students are driven home. If there is no other choice ... be alert.

## 52. WHY DON'T WE SEE HIGH SCHOOL LETTER SWEATERS AND JACKETS AS IN BY-GONE DAYS?

Mostly peer pressure.

Present fashion trends do not include special status for the athlete.

The school letter jacket you purchased fifty years ago for forty dollars now costs two hundred dollars. Students are slow to purchase an expensive item that will be jeered by the other students.

## 53. I COACH A YOUTH TEAM AND PARENTS ARE CONSTANTLY YELLING INSTRUCTIONS AT KIDS DURING GAMES. HOW CAN I STOP THIS?

Many youth sports organization across the country share this concern. One approach is to schedule meetings with parents to discuss the problem and ask parents to sign a support agreement that contains some language about parent involvement and behavior. Some youth organizations have initiated a "silent" attendance policy. All youth sport coaches and parents must understand that little leaguers have a tremendous load to shoulder. They are learning rules and strategies of games that seem complicated while attempting to master the motor skills to play the games.

## 54. IS IT REASONABLE TO ASSUME THAT THOSE WHO WERE THE BEST PLAYERS WOULD BE THE BEST COACHES?

A championship race car driver is not necessarily the best mechanic. Some great coaches never even played the game while some great players find it impossible to teach the game. We might speculate that the proficient athlete lacks patience trying to teach what comes easily to him, while the lesser athlete becomes a student of the sport and more closely examines the fundamentals in the coaching. There is no pattern that always creates a successful coach.

## 55. MY NINE YEAR OLD SON LOVES BASEBALL AND THE COACHES WANT HIM TO PLAY IN SPRING, SUMMER, AND FALL LEAGUES. HOW CAN CONVINCE HIM TO TAKE TIME TO TRY OTHER SPORTS?

If children are to develop an appreciation for art, or classical music, or theater, or professional wrestling, stock car racing and a host of other activities, they must be afforded opportunities of experience. Take your youngster to other sporting events and show an interest in other sports. You can introduce your child to a variety of experiences. You can set the timing ... not the child or the coaches. Nine is too young to put all the eggs in one basket and exclude other possibilities. Talk with the child and encourage multiple experiences.

## 56. OUR FOOTBALL COACH SUSPENDED A STAR PLAYER PRIOR TO A PLAYOFF GAME. MANY PEOPLE FELT THE DISCIPLINE WAS UNFAIR TO OUR SCHOOL. DID THE COACH HAVE OTHER ALTERNATIVES?

Sure ... the coach could have ignored the violation, given a warning, delayed punishment or possibly reduced playing time for the offender. What good are rules if they are only acknowledged when you are sure that the consequences are not threatening to the win column? The suspension of the player should not have been a surprise to anyone once the infraction is known. Every team member and parent should know before the season starts what the athletic code addresses and what team policies are in place. To make an exception for a player makes a mockery of the rules and the integrity of the program.

## 57. WHY DOES MY SON PLAY SO MUCH BETTER IN SOCCER PRACTICE THAN IN GAMES?

The obvious answer might be that the competition is much better in games. However, there are individuals who suffer greatly from contest anxiety that produces frustration and the natural flow for the athlete vanishes. I would suggest that you encourage him to play with a degree of reckless abandon and have fun.

## 58. HOW SHOULD SCHOOL COACHES BE EVALUATED?

The easiest way to evaluate coaches is to compare wins versus losses. It is also the most invalid and unfair manner. There are numerous evaluation instruments used by school administrators in grading teaching and coaching performances. The following elements might be included in the evaluation tool (1) completion of specified duties, (2) communication and relationship skills with staff, athletes, parents, and community, (3) competitiveness of teams, (4) demonstration of emotional stability while under pressure and (5) image projected on behalf of the school district and community.

## 59. ISN'T A FAMILY OUTING OR VACATION AN ACCEPTABLE EXCUSE FOR A CHILD TO MISS SPORT PRACTICES AND GAMES?

A case can be made for this scenario in the elementary programs. This mentality should change once the youngster becomes a team member in middle school and high school. Beginning in middle school there are usually try-outs for teams and, naturally, some youngsters don't make the squad. It is difficult to justify allowing a member to take a vacation from his commitment when others were cut from the team and his teammates stay the course. If a number of families decided to take vacations in the middle of a sport seasons, we would have total collapse of programs. One critical lesson in sport is that of commitment.

## 60. MY SON AND THREE OTHER BOYS GOT IN TROUBLE AT SCHOOL. THEY WERE SUSPENDED A DAY FROM CLASSES. MY SON ALSO WAS BENCHED FOR ONE GAME. WHY DID MY SON GET EXTRA PUNISHMENT BECAUSE HE IS AN ATHLETE? THE OTHER BOYS ARE NOT ON THE TEAM AND ONLY GOT THE SCHOOL SUSPENSION.

Let's examine closely a "healthy" school/sport philosophy. We begin with this premise: Every public school student is entitled to educational opportunities. It is a right. Participation in the extracurricular activities is *not* a right ... but a privilege. Youngsters who engage in sport, band, and other extracurricular activities are made aware that they represent their school in an ambassadorship role. They are not "just another student." The school district, the individual sport and each extra-curricular organization should have printed behavior expectations and consequences for violators. Student-athletes, parents and coaches should discuss all aspects of training rules and team behavior expectations, including punishments for infractions, prior to the season. When one of the ambassadors violates a rule, there must always be judgment used in the analysis. If they are guilty of a rule infraction, there should be no question as to the reaction.

## 61. OUR HIGH SCHOOL VOLLEYBALL TEAM HAS NOT WON VERY MANY GAMES. SHOULDN'T THE COACH LET THE YOUNGER GIRLS PLAY?

It depends upon the philosophy of those making the decision. When teams struggle to win, everyone has a remedy suggestion: "Play the upperclassmen at the varsity and keep the underclassmen together and build a competitive team at that level." or "Fire the upperclassmen and elevate the underclassmen. Take your knocks but get valuable experience for next year."

The decision remains with the coach and it is not an easy decision. The coach must balance the desire to play the best players while still keeping an eye on the future.

## 62. HOW CAN YOUTH LEAGUES ACHIEVE TEAM SKILL BALANCE TO AVOID THE LOPSIDED SCORES?

There is more finagling at youth team drafting meetings than one would find at a major political convention. First, you have a room full of parents jockeying for the best for their own child and, secondly, you usually have a couple of coaches who have greater leverage than the others. To insure better skill balance on youth teams: (1) hold two or more skill evaluation days, (2) invite local school coaches and players to share evaluation input (3) pay particular attention to age and physical maturity in determining a final ratings system.

## 63. MY SON IS THE HIGH SCORER ON THE SOPHOMORE TEAM. THE COACH ELEVATED TWO OTHER SOPHOMORES TO THE VARSITY BUT NOT MY SON. WHY WOULD A COACH DO THIS?

For openers, the coach should have told the teams, and perhaps the public, why he took that action. It is possible that there were certain positions or specific needs at the varsity level and these players seemed to fit the bill. Regardless of my guess, your son should ask the coach if he was considered for the varsity game. Misunderstanding and ill-feelings are magnified when left to the guessing game.

## 64. IS IT PROPER TO THANK A COACH OR BUY HIM A GIFT IN APPRECIATION FOR HIS TIME AND EFFORT?

I believe it is unnecessary to buy gifts. However, a "thank you" is always appreciated. Every coach spends time away from family and other activities as he pursues the responsibilities of coaching. A written thank you note at the close of a season will go far to make his efforts seem worthwhile. Man does not live by bread alone, but sometimes a "hurrah" is food for the spirit.

## 65. WHAT DO YOU DO ABOUT THE COACH'S WIFE? ON EVERY CALL THAT GOES AGAINST OUR TEAM SHE IS SCREAMING AT THE REFEREES. IT'S EMBARRASSING.

Like it or not, and even though not employed by the school district, the coach's spouse and family members are representatives of the school. There are behavior expectations. The administration should share their concerns with the coach in hopes that *he* can correct the undesirable behavior. If this approach does not meet with positive results, it is likely the administration will engage in a more microscopic year-end evaluation of the coach.

## 66. DO YOU THINK IT IS BENEFICIAL FOR MY SON TO PLAY IN YOUTH LEAGUES WITH GIRLS?

Many girls are equally competitive in little league sports. You should not worry that your son's development will be deterred in pre-adolescent coed play. Not until puberty do we begin to notice increased strength development in boys. Co-ed sports beyond the age of about 11 years will create concerns for safety and enjoyment. It is at this time when gender leagues should be the rule.

## 67. DO HIGH SCHOOL COACHES HAVE A RESPONSIBILITY TO ASSIST PLAYERS IN GETTING COLLEGE ATHLETIC SCHOLARSHIPS?

No. There is no contract obligation of high school coaches to secure athletic scholarships for players. However, I firmly believe every high school varsity coach has a moral obligation to assist their players to identify a junior college or college where they might have a realistic opportunity to continue in sport participation. The high school athletes with sufficient skills will be seen by college recruiters. The high school coach can alert some colleges but it is the college coach who determines which players get financial assistance.

## 68. ARE THERE AS MANY COLLEGE ATHLETIC SCHOLARSHIPS FOR FEMALES AS THERE ARE FOR MALES?

Yes. Gender equity laws spelled out in by the federal government have put females on the same page with males when it comes to program opportunities and scholarship offerings. The perception of an imbalance is due to greater media coverage of male sports.

## 69. WHY IS THERE SO MUCH TURNOVER OF COACHES?

There are a number of reasons for coaching turnover: retirement, burn out, better opportunities, and some are forced out. My experiences suggest that some small school administrators embrace a philosophy that identifies aggressive, upward mobility coaching candidates with the belief that their school will benefit (success) from coaches who are looking to build a reputation and move to larger schools. In this scenario the turnover is to be expected.

In the greater scheme it would appear that turnover could be damaging to the desires to build and sustain sport programs. Reducing the coaching turnover seems best combated through effective administrative leadership. This leadership type is found when the top-level school administrators are pro-active with specific goals and plans. In an attempt to create an environment for successful coaching and competitive programs the administration must have a vision. That vision should consider the following three factors: 1) alliances, 2) relationship dynamics, and 3) coaching education. Alliances with administrators and staff are a must. This is best accomplished when the athletic director is an effective conduit. Periodic meetings with coaches and top-level administrators can also do much for creating this alliance. The relationship dynamic issues can become a positive for coaches, players and parents if there is communication. Effective leadership does not leave communication to chance. Instead, specific guidelines are established and a schedule of parent meetings with the athletes are in place each year for every sport. Coaching education must be an on-going mission for the school district. Attendance at sport specific clinics and in-service seminars are important coach-education tools. Coaches must be educated and constantly reminded to anticipate periphery factors, which do impact their programs. The old saying, "everybody talks about the weather but nobody does a thing about it," is not always the case. Some folks take along an umbrella. When administrators assist coaches to anticipate and have the response (game plan), the coaching environment is better and the staying power is greater.

## 70. I USED TO BE A PRETTY GOOD BASKETBALL PLAYER. I SEE SOME OF MY SON'S FRIENDS ON THE TEAM WHO ARE MAKING CONSISTENT ERRORS. CAN I HELP BY GIVING THEM THE BENEFIT OF MY EXPERIENCE?

Probably not.

If you are shooting hoops in the driveway, it's OK. If you are assisting with a youth-league team, it's OK. The situation changes when your son and friends are on a school team in the upper grades. It's probably better to let the coach handle the skill development. You may be undermining the learning progression that the coach is trying to develop.

## 71. ONE OF MY SON'S COACHES WANTS HIM TO CONCENTRATE ON FOOTBALL AND TRACK WHILE ANOTHER COACH IS PUSHING HIM TO PLAY BASKETBALL AND BASEBALL. WHAT SHOULD WE DO?

This is a decision for the family. Your discussion with your son should have him reflect upon his interests and talents. You and your son should make the decision and inform the coaches. This decision should not be deferred to coach who is the better talker.

## 72. I WANT MY DAUGHTER TO PLAY SPORTS BUT I DON'T WANT HER TO GET INJURED. WHICH SPORTS ARE THE SAFEST TO PLAY?

Studies indicate a greater likelihood of injury in softball than bowling. That does not guarantee an injury-free experience in bowling.

There are injury risks in all sport participation. To minimize sport injuries the coach and athlete must pay attention to some important factors: (1) proper equipment (2) safe environment (3) proper warm-up techniques (4) a pre-season physical exam.

Let your daughter play the sports she most enjoys.

## 73. WHAT CONCERNS SHOULD I HAVE ABOUT MY DAUGHTER'S DIET AND WEIGHT DURING THE SPORT SEASON?

The demands of physical training will likely have an effect upon appetite, fatigue, weight, and attitude. Many females undergo drastic body changes during the teen years and these physiological changes must be considered in the proper perspective. Monitor your daughter's diet and activities. Keep your eyes open for significant changes you believe may be negative.

## 74. WHY IS IT THAT SUCCESSFUL MIDDLE SCHOOL TEAMS ENTER HIGH SCHOOL ONLY TO HAVE FAR LESS TEAM SUCCESS?

The answer often lies in "geographical scheduling." Because of transportation, the number of contests and budgets, middle schools usually play schools in close geographic proximity. On the high school side of the equation the territory is expanded due to conference affiliation, invitational tournaments, and state play-off assignments. High school schedules are more competitive than those of the middle school.

This same condition exists with some high schools. The team may dominate their geographic area but have problems when competing with schools from other areas.

## 75. I AM AWARE THAT MY SON AND SOME OF HIS TEAMMATES OFTEN VIOLATE THE SCHOOL ATHLETIC CODE REGARDING ALCOHOL. WHAT SHOULD I DO?

Educators see too many instances where parents become enablers. The parents deny the problem, rationalize the extent of the problem or become co-conspirators. Have you ever witnessed a high school graduation exercise where a lone rose lay on an unoccupied chair signifying a lost life? Often it is a story of teen alcohol usage. Be pro-active on this one. It's not about snitching on kids to get them in trouble; it's about giving youngsters help in avoiding heartbreak and tragedy.

This is a tough topic to broach. You should talk with your son but also recognize that peer pressure is often stronger than parental advice. You can talk with other parents but be prepared for them to resent you for broaching the subject. There are avenues to inform school counselors and coaches without making it a major event. There can be positive approaches taken.

You have the information about the activities of these young people. Ask yourself this ... If you do nothing about it and there is an accident resulting in injury or death to these youngsters, how will you feel? This is not a game ... this is about life.

## 76. EVERY YEAR THERE ARE FATALITIES DURING EARLY SEASON WORKOUTS. WHAT SHOULD THE PARENT AND ATHLETE DO TO PREPARE FOR THE PRACTICES?

Parents should make sure that the pre-season physical examination is complete and thorough. Encourage your youngster to engage in some personal training activities prior to the official start of practice. Make inquiries with the coaching staff as to what measures are planned to re-hydrate athletes during workouts. Also, secure a copy of the school's emergency medical response plan for seriously injured athletes. Monitor your child's diet and rest during the season. The unexpected happens in all walks of life. However, we can avoid many problems through planning.

## 77. MY SON HAS MADE THE BASKETBALL TEAMS THE PAST FEW YEARS BUT DOESN'T GET TO PLAY VERY MUCH. SHOULD I ENCOURAGE HIM TO SEEK OTHER MORE REWARDING INTERESTS?

You are assuming that his roles on these teams have not been rewarding. Your son may be well adjusted to the point that he understands his skills compared to other players and is happy with the contributions he is making.

Most players and parents share a desire for the youngster to have greater playing time and a higher profile on the team. Not everyone can be the star player and some young people accept their role and still benefit from the lessons of hard work, commitment, dedication, team work, and accountability. Talk with your son and let him express his true feelings on his circumstances. Let him make the final decision.

## 78. I THINK THE PRIVATE SECTOR WORK EXPERIENCE IS AS VALUABLE AS THE SPORT EXPERIENCE. AM I WRONG TO EXPECT MY SON TO HOLD A JOB WHILE PLAYING SPORTS?

Many students have to work to assist the home. Some parents may want the child to have a job to teach self-reliance. Assuming the boy can maintain his responsibilities, there is a question of schedule. Practice and travel on weekends and holidays often make a difficult schedule to juggle. A cooperative employer will need to arrange a work schedule.

## 79. OUR HIGH SCHOOL BASKETBALL COACH HAS CLOSED PRACTICES. WHAT'S UP? ISN'T THIS ILLEGAL OR SOMETHING?

No, it's not illegal. Now, let's answer the "what's up?" part. A basketball team may consist of as many as 15 players. If all the parents show up at practice, that's a pretty good gathering, not to mention increased numbers resulting from divorced situations and second families. And why not invite the grandparents? They have an interest. In reality, not all parents would show up at the practices. Those parents whose personal schedule permits free time would possibly be in attendance. Understand that the coaching staff is conducting a class and the best results are forthcoming where there is minimal distraction. Often, youngsters feel uncomfortable when their parents come to practice. They don't do their best because they are worried about what the parent may think. Other youngsters, whose parents cannot be at practice, feel disadvantaged. Better to stay away from practice ... but bring the whole family to the games.

## 80. CAN A PARENT HELP A CHILD DEVELOP COMPETITIVENESS?

I believe every home teaches to some degree an attitude of competitiveness. Add to the mix a few siblings and suddenly the table board games and backyard play is even more intense. Competitiveness breeds an appetite for winning. Encouraging competitiveness in the home may develop the desire to win. Develop good winners, not poor losers.

## 81. WHY DO SOME HIGH SCHOOL COACHES IMPLEMENT TEAM DRESS CODES FOR TEAM TRIPS?

Consider problems that arise without such a code. Some families can afford the expensive designer clothing for their children while others cannot. The clothing represents socio-economic statements that tend to divide the team. If there are no dress code standards we often find players who attempt to distinguish themselves with some very creative apparel. The student-athlete represents more than himself as a member of the team. Athletes are ambassadors for the school and community.

## 82. DO YOU BELIEVE THE MAIN OBJECTIVE IN SPORTS IS TO BUILD CHARACTER?

Character building is certainly one of the objectives in school sports' programs. Character building is nurtured in the family, church, clubs, school organizations, and in every classroom environment. The sport arena does offer a unique setting to teach fairness, commitment, resiliency, determination, and sacrifice, all of which may very well define the ingredients found in character.

There are many worthwhile objectives in sports. The "main" objective may vary for each athlete.

## 83. DO HIGH SCHOOL COACHES RECEIVE "KICKBACK" MONEY FROM COLLEGES WHO RECRUIT THEIR PLAYERS?

It is a violation of the NCAA and small college affiliations to offer money for delivering a recruit. Most efforts designed to enlist the high school coach's favor are little perks.

Colleges recruit coaches just as they do players. The reason is to get the coaches on board to assist in the recruitment of players. If a high school coach wishes to get tickets for college games, tickets seem to be available when you have a good player. The high school coach may get special invitations to clinics and other college events that might not otherwise be forthcoming.

## 84. HOW CAN I EXPECT LEADERSHIP SKILLS TO BE DEVELOPED IN MY DAUGHTER WHEN SHE IS NEVER GIVEN THE OPPORTUNITY TO BE CAPTAIN?

There are two types of leaders. The first is assigned leadership ... that which is appointed. Secondly, leadership is attained through accomplishment.

If your child has never been appointed as a leader there are still ample opportunities to develop leadership skills. Leadership can be earned through such qualities as courage, accomplishment, inspirational abilities, and how other people are treated. Real leadership is earned, not appointed.

## 85. IS IT FAIR TO CHARACTERIZE TODAY'S ATHLETES AS SELF-CENTERED?

It is always unfair to paint with a broad brush of generalizations. Many athletes are aware of their potential to do good works. Many professional athletes become attached to specific charities and lend their support. High school and college athletes are often involved in caring programs. Some athletes have difficulty handling success and expect special treatment. Too often, school coaches are guilty of pampering the better athletes and the self-centered attitude becomes entrenched at an early age. Community and charitable projects teach athletes to be givers. Good coaches spend time and effort orchestrating such opportunities.

## 86. WHAT IS A FAIR PROCESS TO DETERMINE THE RECIPIENT OF A "MOST-VALUABLE-PLAYER" AWARD?

I don't advocate the "most valuable player" elections and I adamantly oppose such an award prior to the high school level. If the award is given in high school then we must agree that only those who see the athletes in both games and practices should have input in the selection scheme. This would mean players and coaches should vote on the recipient. Too often if only players vote it becomes a popularity exercise. If only the coaching staff votes then you void the "team" philosophy. Coaches and players should decide the MVP after careful examination of statistical categories. I always told players and coaches that when voting on these awards ask yourself a simple question: If we were choosing sides to play a pick-up game, which person would you pick first? That's likely the MVP.

## 87. MUST I SIGN A PARENT CONSENT FORM TO AN ATHLETIC CODE WHEN I DO NOT AGREE TO SOME STATEMENTS?

A parent is not compelled to sign anything. However, your child may be denied the privilege of sport competition. Note the word privilege. Your child has a right to a (public) school education but the opportunity to participate in extra-curricular programs has expectations beyond those of the general school population. Share your concerns about the consent form with the coach or administrators. Good communication usually resolves impasses.

## 88. WHY DO SOME COACHES SAY HURTFUL THINGS ABOUT PLAYERS WHEN BEING INTERVIEWED BY THE PRESS?

There is no good excuse for this happening. The reason usually stems from a lack of time between an emotional game and the interview. Coaches would be wise to take some time for introspection and conversation with assistant coaches before they engage the media

57

Occasionally, a poor coach will look for a scapegoat for a loss.

## 89. HOW CAN I MINIMIZE EXCUSE MAKING AMONG MY LITTLE LEAGUE PLAYERS?

None of us, wants to be at fault. It's our nature to first look to place blame when things go awry. "Who is going to like me if I screw up."

To help youngsters not to make excuses, you must understand where they are coming from and where you would like to take them. Little kids playing games are caught up in social acceptance. Point out to youngsters, "Even the greatest players make errors. When mistakes are made it serves no good purpose to assign blame but it does has a negative effect. Get ready for the next play." If finger-pointing becomes hurtful then more drastic measures must be taken with the offender.

## 90. WHAT CAN I DO WHEN THE HIGH SCHOOL COACH PLAYS MY SON IN A POSITION NOT SUITED FOR HIM?

Many parents today coached their children in youth programs and have a sense and desire for their son's best position in a particular sport. The parent may be correct in the analysis. If you feel strongly about the situation, encourage your son to talk with the coach about the matter. The issue should be discussed between player and coach. Keep in mind that every parent is looking at the team through biased eyes. The wise coach should attempt to put the best people in a line-up that enhances the competitiveness of the team. Sometimes a player with generally good skills in a sport may be asked to play out of position to allow a position-specific skilled player to be in the line-up.

## 91. WHY DO SOME COACHES BUILD THEIR TEAMS AROUND ONE OR TWO STAR PLAYERS?

Any good team is comprised of players who understand and accept their roles. This certainly means that some offensive and defensive designs in the team approach may be centered on the most prolific players. I knew the name of the orthopedic surgeon who did my back surgery and I thanked him for pain relief. Although I don't know the support cast connected with the operation, I am none-the-less grateful for their expertise and contribution. Coaches should always point out to the team and the media the efforts and importance of each member.

## 92. WHY CAN A STUDENT TRANSFER FROM THE PRIVATE SCHOOL IN OUR TOWN TO THE PUBLIC SCHOOL AND BE ELIGIBLE? MY DAUGHTER MUST SIT OUT A YEAR IF SHE TRANSFERS FROM THE PUBLIC TO THE PRIVATE SCHOOL?

Across the nation many state high school associations have toiled with the transfer issue and the recruitment of athletes. The problem boils down to a question of public school attendance boundaries versus the private school's lack of attendance boundaries. Public schools must verify that students playing on their athletic teams do live within the school district. To minimize the enticement of athletes from public schools to the private schools, many state associations have enacted by-laws that carry an ineligibility clause for a time period. On the other hand, since the private schools have no boundary restrictions, the transfer from private school to public school is not penalized as long as the student does reside in the public school's district. The student who lives in the district is entitled to go to the public school. It is important that parents be aware of state association residence factors if contemplating a school change.

## 93. IS IT NECESSARY FOR THESE YOUTH PROGRAMS TO HAVE THE ENDLESS PARADE OF FUND RAISING PROJECTS?

We all have purchased our share of over-priced candy bars from towhead lads in uniform. The reality in funding youth sports is obvious. It is an expensive proposition. Even after local businesses contribute sponsorship money there remains expense. Usually, the only remaining options are fund raising schemes. Some observers believe there is a positive result of youngsters trying to help themselves.

## 94. WHY IS MY DAUGHTER SO UPTIGHT PRIOR TO A VOLLEYBALL GAME WHEN SHE HAS BEEN THE TOP PLAYER FOR THREE YEARS?

There is an anxiety factor that can plague top performing athletes. Imagine for the moment that year after year, game in and game out, you perform at a high level of proficiency. You become aware that many people have developed high expectations in your play. Your teammates look to you in crucial game moments, your coach has orchestrated plays around your skills and fans have been spoiled by your performance. Would you not be anxious? Most all highly skilled athletes have pre-games anxiety but it fades quickly when the contest begins and the athlete gets into a flow. You might tell your daughter that you understand some of the pressures she may be feeling. Such a comment might be appreciated by her.

## 95. MY SON'S SOCCER TEAM IS PLAYING ON THE SAME DAY THAT THE HIGH SCHOOL HOMECOMING COURT IS BEING HONORED. SHOULD HE CHOOSE TO PLAY SOCCER OR BE RECOGNIZED AS A COURT MEMBER?

The answer should be obvious … but surprisingly it is not. Your son and some 25 or 30 soccer players have been involved in preparation and competition for the entire season. Leaving his soccer team to be recognized in the homecoming ceremony would demonstrate a selfish motive. He made a commitment to be part of the team … he should be with them.

## 96. WHAT CAN I DO WHEN MY FATHER, REGARDLESS HOW I PLAY, ALWAYS POINTS OUT THINGS I COULD HAVE DONE BETTER IN THE GAME?

Ask your father to list the good things you do in contests as well as the things that could be improved. If parents and young athletes are to have a good sport experience there must be open and free conversation. No one should be guessing what the other one is thinking. Often, parents fear that their athlete will get a big head over achievements and thus not improve. Parents can have too great expectations and that should be discussed. The athlete must be prepared to handle both the positive and corrective statements. It is critical that parent-child talk is neither all praise nor all criticism.

## 97. ARE WE BEING SELFISH PARENTS IF WE WANT OUR DAUGHTER TO GO TO A COLLEGE NEARER HOME SO WE CAN SEE HER PLAY SPORTS?

If she goes to a college of your choice, you risk carrying the blame if things don't go well. Let her select the college she wishes to attend after family discussion regarding financial ability, sports competition, and degree offerings. This is a major decision in every young person's life and it must have her name all over the choice.

## 98. I FEAR THAT MY THREE YEAR OLD SON WILL NOT PLAY SPORTS. WHAT CAN I DO TO MOVE HIM IN THE SPORT DIRECTION?

Relax. It is not unusual to see more than one golfer in a family, more than one fisherman in a family, or more than one coin collector in a family. Youngsters tend to gravitate to the activities that they experience with the family. Your interests will come through clearly to your son. Be careful. The one certain thing which will drive him away from sport is the absence of fun.

## 99. I'M NOT A FASHION FREAK BUT OUR COACH ON THE SIDELINE LOOKS LIKE A RAG PILE. SHOULD I SAY SOMETHING TO HIM ABOUT HIS IMAGE?

Obviously his mother doesn't attend the games. If the appearance of the coach causes you concern you might broach the subject with a school administrator in private. Most school districts have a policy regarding faculty dress and, if the administrator agrees, the matter will likely be shared with the coach.

### End